Travel in the Artist's Footsteps!

Susan Rodriguez

CrystalProductions
Glenview, Illinois

 In loving memory of Pat Meehan, spirited traveler, superb art teacher, and dear friend who will live in our hearts forever.

Acknowledgements

Enormous thanks to Melissa Calder–aka Tonto–without whom the author would have been the Lost Ranger! Merci Beaucoup to Kelly Badeau, Amy Woodworth, and to Lorry Hubbard and Tom Hubbard! Many thanks to my art teacher friends and students for their contributions and encouragement: Stacy Zellner, May Sam, Amy Jared, Krissy Krygiel-Evans, Connie Dauval, Beth Bell, Katy Morris, Mike Mann, Sheryl Antinoff, Zahmu Sankofa, Leora Chwalow, "Mr. Bags," Joanne Harris, and the Siebert family. Special thanks and love to Paul and Ilana Blumenthal. Appreciation to the Philadelphia Sketch Club, and to Stephanie Okupniak-Vaughan. Gratitude to The Professional Institute for Educators at UARTS, especially Karyn Tufarolo et al; Art Education students and to our Chair, Randy Granger. I'd like to thank Barbara Bassett at Philadelphia Museum of Art, and Al Gury at Pennsylvania Academy of the Fine Arts, and to all others who are in between the lines of this book.

Cover: Claude Monet, *The Gare Saint-Lazare (Suburban Lines)*, 1877; pencil; 10 x 13⅖ inches (25.5 x 34 cm). © 2008 Dover Publications, Inc. Claude Monet, *The Road Bridge at Argenteuil*, 1874; oil on canvas; 24 x 32 inches (61.2 x 81.3 cm). © 2008 Dover Publications, Inc.

Library of Congress Cataloging-in-Publication Data

Rodriguez, Susan, 1944-
 Travels with Monet : travel in the artist's footsteps / Susan Rodriguez. — 1st ed.
    p. cm.
 ISBN 978-1-56290-664-1
 1. Monet, Claude, 1840-1926—Juvenile literature. I. Monet, Claude, 1840-1926. II. Title.

ND553.M7R58 2010
759.4dc22

2010020317

Copyright © 2010 by Crystal Productions Co.
All Rights Reserved

ISBN 978-1-56290-664-1
Printed in Hong Kong

Itinerary

Water, Water Everywhere...and Claude Monet to Paint It!	4
Sketching and Seaports: The Days of Claude Monet	5
Bonjour Paris!	6-7
Monet in Paris	8-9
The Escape Artists	10
Impressionism Stuns Paris!	11
Full Steam Ahead	12
1874: An Important Year for the Impressionists	13
Japan, Mon Amour	14
How Does Your Garden Grow?	15
The Fleeting Moment	16-17
"The Seine Is My Studio"	18-19
Following Monsieur Monet...North to South	20-21
Giverny, Japan, and the Series Paintings	22-23
Cathedrals and Japanese Gardens	24-25
The Intrepid Traveler	26-27
The Sistine Chapel of Impressionism	28-29
Activity Pond	30-31

Water, Water Everywhere... and Claude Monet to Paint It!

Claude Oscar Monet was born in Paris in 1840 near the river Seine. He grew up in Le Havre in Normandy, the place where the mouth of the River Seine meets the English Channel in Northern France. Monet had a happy, adventurous childhood by the sea.

His artistic enthusiasm and outgoing nature appeared early in life. He was hardly an ideal student and doodled in the margins of his notebooks. "I was born undisciplined," admitted Monet.

Eugène Boudin, *Beach Sceneat Trouville*, 1863. Oil on wood, 13 11/16 x 22 5/8 inches (34.8 x 57.5 cm 0 © 2006 Dover Publications, Inc.

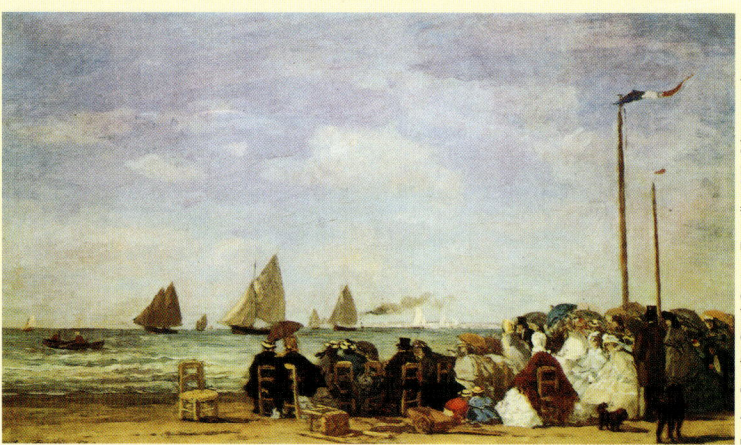

As you can see in Beach Scene at Trouville, the "Age of Tourism" begins!

One day Boudin said to me "Learn to draw well and appreciate the sea, the light, the blue sky." I took his advice. — Claude Monet

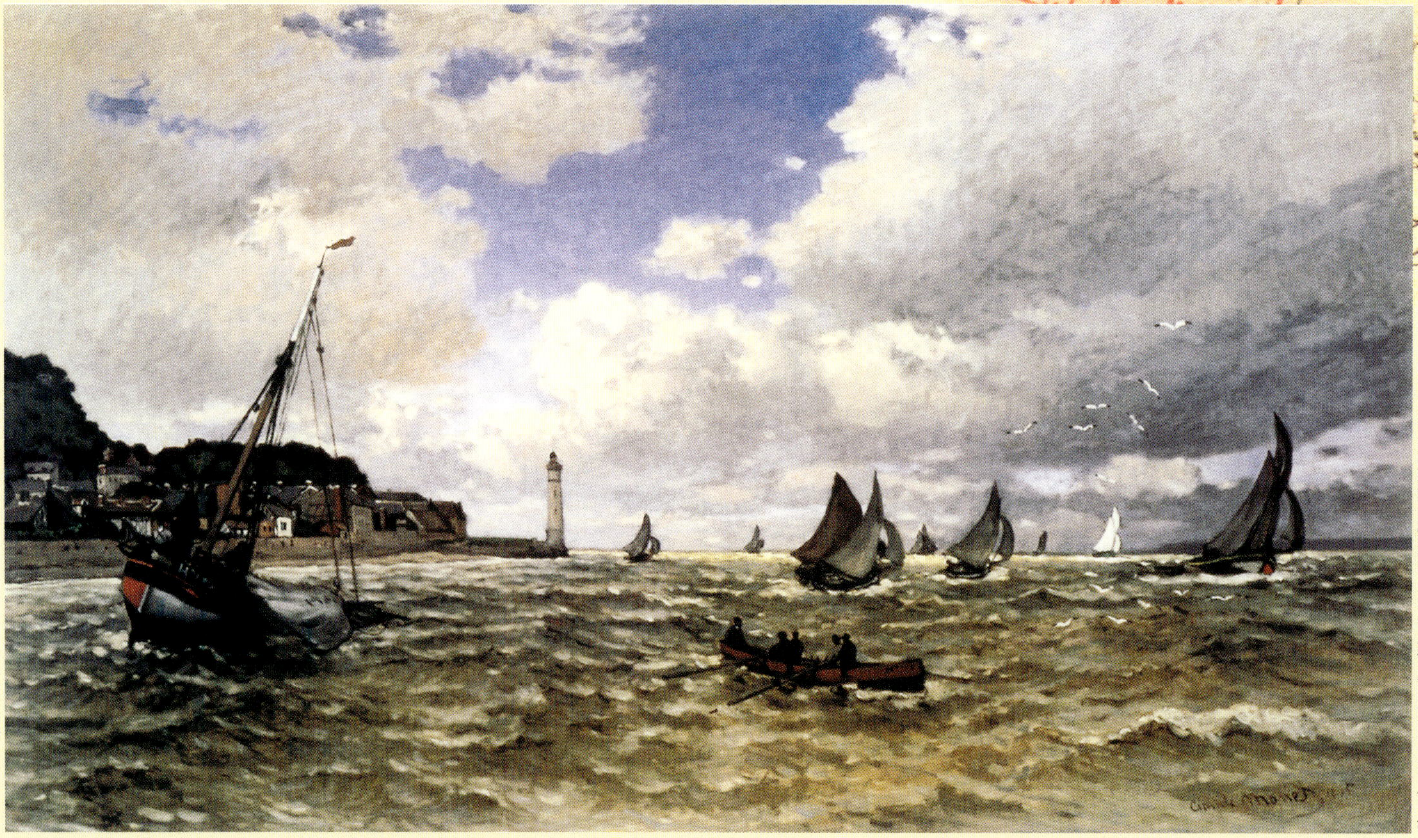

Claude Monet, *Mouth of the Seine at Honfleur*, 1865; oil on canvas; 35 1/4 x 59 1/4 inches (89.5 x 150.5 cm). © 2008 Dover Publications, Inc.

One might say that Monet was destined to become the most admired painter of the 19th century. There is no doubt that his talent, like his spirit and appetite for life, was enormous. Yet he was also in the right place at the right time. It so happened that artist Eugène Boudin — sometimes called "the world's littlest Impressionist" — lived nearby. Other artists, like Gustave Courbet, an outdoor painter and naturalist, loved the coast of Normandy and visited frequently.

Sketching and Seaports: The Days of Claude Monet

Local legend has it that young Monet's caricatures appeared in the town's art supply and frame shop window to the enjoyment of the town folk, who followed the pictures as they were replaced each week in a gold frame. Boudin — who painted en plein air (in open air) — saw Monet's amusing caricatures at the shop. He immediately recognized exceptional creativity. Boudin introduced Monet to en plein air painting and became his mentor.

"Suddenly it was as if a veil had been torn away…I understood what painting could be," stated Monet. As a result, he would discover his interest: water in its many manifestations…sky, light, color, and the changing atmosphere. He would never be too far away from water no matter where he lived or traveled.

Claude Monet, 1860. Photo: Carjat

Caricature was very popular in France during Monet's era. Students can draw a portrait of a famous person, or do a self-portrait. Remember to exaggerate the facial features and hair!

Claude Monet, Caricature of Jules Didier, "Butterfly Man," c. 1858; pencil and watercolor on paper; 24¼ x 17 inches. © 2008 Dover Publications, Inc.

- 🎨 Paint or sketch a miniature outdoor scene.
- 🎨 Cut paper into the shape of a palette to create a palette shaped landscape or seascape (see photo at left).

The seaport of Honfleur where Monet visited with painters Boudin, Bazille, and Jongkind in 1864, when it was still a fishing village. Today it is an artist's delight!

See Activity Pond pages 30-31 for more ideas

Bonjour Paris!

It was Boudin who encouraged Monet to go to Paris to study. In 1859, Monet entered the Academie Suisse, named for its founder, Charles Suisse. Many famous artists attended this Atelier (ah-tahl-*yay*) at one time or another — Manet, Pissarro, Cézanne, and Monet, whose parents worried that it wasn't "serious" enough for him. Military service in Algeria soon ensued. After a short stint, Monet became ill with typhoid fever and was discharged to Le Havre. He painted some more seascapes, then headed to Paris, where he shared a flat with fellow artist Frédéric Bazille. He also met Camille Doncieux, an artist's model who would later become his wife.

A French franc note featuring Cézanne's art. What a great idea!

Paris, while becoming modern and sophisticated, still had its traditions. In Charles Gleyre's Atelier, academic painting was strongly upheld. Subjects such as historical events, Greek mythology, and an occasional impersonal scene were considered the height of taste for the yearly Salon exhibit. Monet was once again a student, confronting rules that did not necessarily agree with his point of view.

Art picnic anyone?
See page 30 for instructions

In 1862 a group was forming at Charles Gleyre's studio — Pierre-Auguste Renoir, Alfred Sisley, Frédéric Bazille, and Claude Monet. They shared ideas at cafés and went on "outdoor" painting excursions, favoring the forest of Fontainebleau outside Paris. The forests were also "discovered" by artist Gustave Courbet, leader of the naturalist movement and rebel against Academy conformity. The group had yet to shake things up with the radical art movement that would be called Impressionism.

This large painting is a study for an even larger one that Monet never completed. Monet's friend Bazille posed three times: for the man lying down, and for those standing on the left and in the center. Camille Doncieux, Monet's wife, also appears in this painting. Monet dug a ditch to accommodate large paintings so that he could paint the top portion when he worked outdoors. Who is that man behind the tree?

Claude Monet, *Luncheon on the Grass (Déjeuner sur l'herbe)*, 1865–1866. Pushkin Museum of Fine Arts, Moscow, Russia. Photo Credit: Scala / Art Resource, NY

The young man who loved water, boats and nature also loved flower gardens—particularly water lilies.

Monet sketched this idea before attempting the full scale study below.

When Monet came to Paris, the way for an artist to become famous was to be accepted by the Official Salon under Emperor Napoleon III. The sheer volume and size of both the paintings themselves and the event — thousands of huge paintings were submitted — was staggering! An artist's career could easily be made or crushed. Imagine dragging canvases twice your size to be judged by a fussy jury. If they didn't like your work, the back of the canvas would be stamped in oversized letters, REJECTED. There was nothing delicate about this process. Not easily intimidated, Monet tried his hand at the Salon. To his utter amazement, in 1866, he learned that three paintings he submitted were ACCEPTED! He was flattered, but he soon dispensed with Salon-style painting, having proved he had the skills to meet their conventional standards. He was also rejected numerous times.

Monet would travel far and wide, but never forget to draw!

Sketch based on Monet's painting River Scene at Bennecourt, 1868

Don't forget your sketchbook. Bring it everywhere you travel!

MONET IN PARIS

The Paris Monet inhabited was the picture of modernity. In the previous decade, Paris was still a medieval city with narrow walkways and unpleasant sanitation problems. It was not the City of Lights — far from it. Under the directive of Napoleon III's architect, Baron Haussmann, old Paris was demolished. In its place appeared grand boulevards, city parks, the Opera, and the Louvre Palace. The city plan was dazzling and elegant. This was the Paris of Édouard Manet, the urbane Parisian whose paintings captured scenes of modern life, such as the open air concerts at the Tuileries Gardens and corner tables at outdoor cafés.

Manet is sometimes referred to as "the grandfather of Impressionism," although he never exhibited with the group. He anticipated them in his direct painting methods and was established as a progressive master. When Monet's paintings appeared at the Salon, they puzzled everyone. Understandably, since the painters' last names were spelled the same except for one vowel. Monet and Manet spent time together and learned from each other. Both artists were revolutionary in their own right. Manet had notorious difficulties with the Salon. To add to the confusion, Monet responded to Manet's *Luncheon on the Grass* with his own version of the theme. Manet, as a recognized painter of modern life, is shown in Fantin-Latour's *Studio at Batignolles* (right) as a glowing prophet, surrounded by his disciples, including Renoir, Bazille, and Monet.

Manet's Music in the Tuileries Gardens is very much inspired by photography, for it appears frozen like a snapshot. The painting includes portraits of many of Manet's author, artist, and musician friends, and even includes a self-portrait on the far left.

Manet is depicted as a glowing prophet in this painting, surrounded by his disciples.

Henri Fantin Latour, *Studio at Batignolles*, 1870. Oil on canvas, 204 x 237.5 cm. Photo: Hervé Lewandowski. Musée d'Orsay, Paris, France. Photo Credit: Réunion des Musées Nationaux / Art Resource, NY

Manet sits at the center of this painting, palette in hand, painting a portrait of artist and critic Zacharie Astruc (seated). Watching Manet paint (back left) is Otto Schoelderer, a German artist, and Renoir. Emile Zola, a famous writer, is at the center. Behind Zola is a musician named Maitre. Tall, bearded, and handsome stands Frédéric Bazille (in profile), and behind him, his dear friend Monet. This picture was shown in the Salon of 1870, the same year the Franco-Prussian war broke out, turning the streets of Paris into a battleground. The talented Bazille was killed in action. Monet had begged him not to enlist. His friends deeply mourned their loss.

Édouard Manet, *Music in the Tuileries Gardens*, 1862. Oil on canvas, 76.2 x 118.1 cm. Sir Hugh Lane Bequest, 1917 (NG3260). National Gallery, London. Photo Credit: © National Gallery, London / Art Resource, NY

Gustave Caillebotte, *A Paris Street, Rain* (detail), 1877.
Caillebotte exhibited in five of the eight Impressionist exhibits.

Gustave Caillebotte, *A Paris Street, Rain*. 1877. Art Institute, Chicago, IL. Photo Credit: Erich Lessing / Art Resource, NY

Concert ticket please! Have a seat... draw a chair, or sculpt one with wire!

THE ESCAPE ARTISTS

The year of 1870 was of significance to Monet. He married his great love, Camille. They had a son, Jean. The Monet family joined artists Camille Pissarro and Alfred Sisley in London. Paris suffered extensive damage from the Franco-Prussian war, making London a more reasonable city in which to live. For Monet's art, London had the Houses of Parliament, silhouetted above the River Thames.

IDEA What's a frog pond without François the frog? Use construction paper, scissors, glue, and wiggle eyes. C'est tout!

Claude Monet, *Bathers at La Grenouillère*, 1869, oil on canvas; 28¾ x 36¼ (73 x 92 cm). © 2008 Dover Publications, Inc.

Growing closer to their being labeled as "Impressionists," the artists while in London seemed further inspired in that direction. Monet who had long been intrigued by weather in its many moods was thrilled with London's fog, and its effects. Here is the beginning of his work in series. Seeing English painter J.M.W. Turner's canvases featuring "tinted steam" inspired Monet… trains, steamboats, industry on the working river. If industrialized France wasn't before him, London would do just fine. Another noteworthy point about Monet in London is his acquaintance with French art dealer Paul Durand-Ruel who became an advocate of Monet's work. Monet left London with some patronage, painting his way through Zaandam, then Amsterdam, producing many new canvasses to record his travels.

Claude Monet, *The Thames Below Westminster*, about 1871. Oil on canvas, 47 x 72.5 cm. Bequeathed by Lord Astor of Hever, 1971 (NG6399). National Gallery, London, Great Britain. Photo Credit: © National Gallery, London / Art Resource, NY

Claude Monet, *Windmill at Zaandam*, 1871. Oil on canvas, 48 x 73.5. Ny Carlsberg Glyptotek, Copenhagen, Denmark. Photo Credit: Erich Lessing / Art Resource, NY

Le Petit Journal illustré

HEBDOMADAIRE
61, rue Lafayette, Paris

PRIX : 0 fr. 30
26 Avril 1874

IMPRESSIONISM STUNS PARIS!

Claude Monet, *Impression, Sunrise*, 1872, oil on canvas; 18⅞ x 24¼ inches (48 x 63 cm); © 2008 Dover Publications, Inc.

April 26, 1874: The First "Impressionist" Exhibit is Held

It is hard for us to understand today why these paintings that we call Impressionism were so shocking to the public in 1874. At that time, people were accustomed to paintings with highly polished surfaces, and glorified subject matter. Impressionism, which took its name from Monet's Impression, Sunrise, presented images that were not only ordinary, they were judged hardly worthy of attention. The public expected art to elevate them—how could factories belching soot compare to heroes of mythology? To add insult to injury, the Impressionists made no effort to hide their brushstrokes—they flaunted them! These works looked unfinished. In fact, they were, for the most part, less developed than previous artists' preliminary studies! As if that weren't enough, the bright colors seemed gaudy and garish to eyes that were used to canvases using somber brown, black, and earth tones.

The Industrial Revolution in itself was an engine that would drive Impressionism. Foremost, trains enabled travel…especially to leisure spots (a new concept) along the Seine River, such as La Grenouillere — The Frog Pond (see Froggie on page 10). Portable paint tubes, a new product, made outdoor painting accessible at last. "Colors in tubes allowed us to paint totally from nature. Without color in tubes, there would be no Cézanne, no Pissarro, and no Impressionism," quoted Renoir. And now, with the speed of a steam train rolling along the French countryside, next stop: Impressionism!

Full Steam Ahead

Many artists lived near the Gare Saint-Lazare during the 1870s and 1880s. It was also the most popular train station for the weekend excursions which were becoming so popular.

Monet was fascinated with the elements of the atmosphere. Steam was no exception. One day Monet and Renoir visited Gare Saint Lazare train station. "Good day, Monsieur," said Monet, who was dressed elegantly in spite of his financial difficulties. He handed the Station Master his card. "I have been considering which train stations to paint in Paris, and it is now between you and the Gare du Nord. Yours has more character. Of course, you will halt all the trains and fire up the boilers if you wish to be selected." The Station Master, impressed by Monet's authority, agreed at once. Renoir was amazed by Monet's sheer nerve. "I wouldn't even try that (stunt) in front of a grocery store," said Renoir.

How did Impressionism arrive?

Impressionism, by contemporary standards, is the most popular movement in art history. Without the leadership of Claude Monet, it would have been difficult if not impossible for the group to survive, grow, and realize acceptance for their extraordinary vision. Like any other major change in society, a convergence of events enabled Impressionism. The Industrial Revolution put a sense of change in the air. Train networks allowed people who previously did not take weekend excursions to discover the idea of recreation. No longer for the upper class only, working class Parisians enjoyed boat rentals, concerts, parks, and picnics. They would become a subject source for the Impressionists, particularly Renoir.

Japanese prints flooded into Paris after the reopening of trade with Japan after hundreds of years of isolation from the West. The inventive compositions, use of brilliant color and pattern, love of nature, focus on amusements, theater, and the use of cropping — which coincided with the advent of photography — European artists were inspired! Evidence of Japanese influence was everywhere in Paris.

Impressionism was shaped by these events, yet its existence was principally viewed as a reaction against the academic painting style of the Salon. This was true, but not entirely. Art critic Théodore Duret explained: "The Impressionists did not grow like mushrooms. They are the descendants of the naturalist painters. Their forefathers are Corot, Courbet, and Manet. The art of painting is indebted to these three masters for introducing simple techniques and spontaneous methods of painting…the Impressionists received all this from their predecessors and were also influenced by Japanese art."

1874: An Important Year for the Impressionists

Édouard Manet, *The Monet Family in Their Garden at Argenteuil*, 1874. Oil on canvas, 24 x 39 1/4 in. (61 x 99.7 cm). Bequest of Joan Whitney Payson, 1975 (1976.201.14). The Metropolitan Museum of Art, New York, NY. Image copyright ©The Metropolitan Museum of Art / Art Resource, NY

Monet lived with his young family at Argenteuil, a small, picturesque town along the Seine. In the summer following their first Impessionist show, Monet invited his artist friends to his country home. Manet joined the group outdoors to create this painting in an Impressionist manner with a bright palette.

IDEA Have you ever tried to paint a painting inside a painting? See the Activity Pond for suggestions.

The year of 1874 was certainly an exciting one for Monet and his friends. The first exhibit of "the Independents" was held in the vacated studios of Felix Nadar, pioneer in the invention of photography. Among the initial artists who exhibited were Eugene Boudin, Marie Bracquemond, Paul Cézanne, Edgar Degas, Claude Monet, Berthe Morisot, Camille Pissarro, Pierre-Auguste Renoir, and Alfred Sisley. There would be eight exhibits in all between 1874 and 1886. Many art luminaries' work would appear at the other shows — Paul Gauguin, Gustave Caillebotte, Jean-François Millet, and Mary Cassatt, for example. Pissarro never missed an exhibit and later experimented with Pointillism, a scientifically influenced technique developed by Georges Seurat. When Seurat exhibited his first Pointillistic work in 1886, it marked a shift away from Impressionism and its last group exhibit.

Édouard Manet, *Monet in his Floating Studio*, 1874. Oil on canvas, 82.7 x 105 cm. Neue Pinakothek, Bayerische Staatsgemaeldesammlungen, Munich, Germany. Photo Credit: Bildarchiv Preussischer Kulturbesitz / Art Resource, NY

Yes, it's a little confusing. This painting by Édouard Manet shows Monet painting from his studio boat. The boat enabled Monet to paint from the water and to capture the reflections on the water at different times. His wife Camille in the cabin looks much like a Geisha from a Japanese print.

JAPAN, MON AMOUR

Claude Monet, *The Japanese Woman*, 1875; oil on canvas; 91¼ x 56 (231.7 x 142.2 cm). © 2008 Dover Publications, Inc.

Monet, like most of his Impressionist friends, was enamored with the art of the Japanese woodblock print. Little shops opened all over Paris offering imported goods such as fans, screens, and a variety of kimonos. Monet posed his wife Camille in a red kimono and a blonde wig. The painting was popular and sold quickly. Monet is rumored to have remarked that he felt sorry for the buyer since he dismissed the painting as "trash." He must have been swept up in The Great Wave of "Japonisme" (Jah-poh-*neez*-meh), as Japanese decorative art was known in France. Monet would fully embrace Japanese sensibilities in his garden at Giverny.

Are you a Fan of Japan? Note the circular fans on the wall. These fans are known as Uchiwa, based on their shape (compare with folded fan held by Camille). Use a humble paper plate…glue or tape paint mixing sticks to the back. Draw or paint a flower, a portrait, or a mountain – subjects from nature work naturally!

A Lively Idea: Find a volunteer to pose in a kimono for your class! It might seem as though Monet's painting has come to life (it's "tableau vivant," meaning "living painting").

How Does Your Garden Grow?

Claude Monet, *The Artist's Garden at Vétheuil*, 1880, oil on canvas; 59⅝ x 47⅞ inches (151.5 x 121 cm). © 2008 Dover Publications, Inc.

In 1880, Monet was forty years old. Much had happened in his life. He lost his beloved Camille to illness. After times of devastating poverty, the great artist began achieving success. Art historian Théodore Duret writes once again about Monet: "Monet has devoted the larger part of his career in painting to the area around Paris. He has lived, successively, in Argenteuil and Vétheuil where the Seine provided him with the capricious, changeable waterscape of which he is especially fond. He also made frequent trips to the Channel coast and has painted in England and Holland. He has already produced a considerable body of work extremely varied in both site and subject…every kind of landscape, seascape, snow effects…pictures that depict garden flowers in all their vivacity. No artist has been less monotonous."

IDEA

Have you met Redouté? Why not use botanical illustrations as inspiration for flower watercolor paintings?

Monet treasured flower books. He owned a large collection. A wonderful botanical illustrator to the court of Marie-Antoinette was Pierre-Joseph Redouté.

"I perhaps owe becoming a painter to flowers."
— Claude Monet

The Fleeting Moment

This painting is of Camille, five years before her death. Does Monet anticipate her disappearance with this painting? She looks like a scarf in the wind. It is eloquent. She is elevated on a hillside, shadows visually lifting her and their son Jean, standing behind her. The breeze blows against her as clouds move silently across the sky. It is a fleeting moment in time — forever captured by Monet — and an icon of Impressionism.

Claude Monet, *Woman with a Parasol—Madame Monet (Camille) and Her Son*, 1875; oil on canvas; 39½ x 32 inches (100 x 81 cm). © 2008 Dover Publications, Inc.

IDEA

Cloud paintings: Clouds, like snowflakes, are not all alike. There are different types, such as cumulus (big, white, fluffy), cirrus (wispy and high in the sky), stratus (thin layer covering the sky). As an activity, use a white crayon to draw cloud formations on white paper (of course it will be difficult to see). Here is the fun part: apply blue watercolor to the entire surface and watch the clouds appear. You can also use this technique to create a snowscape. Emphasize the falling snow rather than the snow on the ground. Think about the quality of the snowflakes. Are they falling fast and icy, soft and puffy, or fine, like light rain? Your picture will reveal the answer.

Claude Monet, *Poppy Field at Argenteuil*, 1873; oil on canvas; 24⅜ x 32 inches (62.5 x 81.3 cm). © 2008 Dover Publications, Inc.

There are places that mark Monet's life and artistic growth. Among them are Argenteuil (Ar-zhan-teh) and Vétheuil (Vay-teh). In 1878, his second son, Michel, was born. Camille was in very poor health. The Monets moved in with friends Alice and Ernest Hoschedé. Much to Monet's great sadness, Camille passed away in 1879 at the age of 32. Camille and their sons are remembered in many of Monet's most famous paintings. The countryside glimmers with red poppies in this beautiful, somewhat mysterious scene.

"Color is my day-long obsession, joy, and torment" — Claude Monet

Argenteuil and Vétheuil are both charming towns near the river Seine. Both offered Monet ample views to paint outdoors. Monet embodied the characteristics of Impressionism. He painted in all weather conditions, embraced atmospheric change, and loved nature — water, sky, wind, and earth. Unlike his friends Renoir and Manet, Monet was not drawn to Parisian cabaret and café scenes. Monet was an Outdoor Man!

Claude Monet, *The Road in Vétheuil in Winter*, 1879; oil on canvas. © 2008 Dover Publications, Inc.

"The Seine Is My Studio"

The River Seine is said to never fail to delight the traveler. It is best known as it flows through the city of Paris, often regarded as the birthplace of Impressionism and the epicenter of art and culture. Impressionists such as Pissarro, Degas, Renoir, and Manet favored city scenes and studies of Parisians. As for Monet, a native-born Parisian, the Seine would guide his restless artistic drive — from Le Havre in Normandy to Giverny. He would journey in France, Italy, England, Switzerland, the Netherlands, Norway, Algeria, and Spain. Some of these locations would provide immediate interest; others, he would carry in his memory for later use. Yet, it was the River Seine and its country retreats that would continue to beckon the artist. Where he traveled and where he lived provided the ingredients for Monet's art. Location equals inspiration!

Smile, and say "Fromage!"

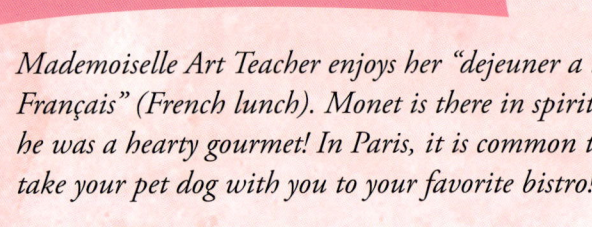

What, no cats?

Mademoiselle Art Teacher enjoys her "dejeuner a la Français" (French lunch). Monet is there in spirit, for he was a hearty gourmet! In Paris, it is common to take your pet dog with you to your favorite bistro!

No One Paints Water Like Monet!

Claude Monet, *The Road Bridge at Argenteuil*, 1874; oil on canvas; 24 x 32 inches (61.2 x 81.3 cm); © 2008 Dover Publications, Inc.

IDEA

Why not grab a camera or use your cell phone to take a snapshot of a spot that would have appealed to Monet? Print it, then apply bright, Impressionist tones to enhance it with colored pencils or other medium of your choosing. Feel free to photocopy the Philadelphia bridge shown here, and follow the instructions as stated.

Following Monsieur Monet…

Nice, (sounds like niece) in the south of France, "the Paris of the Riviera." Many artists worked and lived in the south of France — Renoir, Cézanne, and later Matisse, Picasso, and Chagall.

Allow Monet and his travels to transport you through art! When Monet traveled, it was not only for amusement. He wanted to understand the character of place and time. He endured all sorts of climates so he could achieve his paintings, much like a mountain climber strives to reach the summit.

Monet tried to capture the distinct, defining features of land and sea. If it were a hot day, he wanted you to feel that sensation through his painting, as in the Italian resort town of Bordighera where he spent three months. He expressed his delight — as well as frustrations with the palm trees — in letters to his second wife Alice. The colors he selected helped him give a humid haziness to the canvas suggesting summer temperatures.

Monet also traveled to the French Riviera, as shown in *La Corniche de Monaco*. It is quite a calm scene when compared to one of his many images of beloved Etretat, on the coast of the Atlantic Ocean in Normandy (see his letter to Alice on the following page).

La Corniche de Monaco, a lookout point on the French Riviera on the coast of the Mediterranean Sea.

Bordighera, a resort town in Italy.

North to South

IDEA Mail Art! See Activity Pond on pages 30 and 31

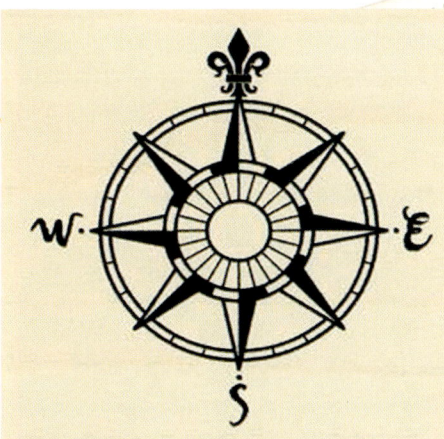

My Dear Alice,

I was hard at work beneath the cliff, well sheltered from the wind, convinced that the tide was drawing out. I took no notice of the waves which came and fell a few feet away from me. In short, absorbed as I was, I didn't see a huge wave coming, it threw me against the cliff, and I was tossed about in its wake along with all my materials...the worst of it was that I lost my painting which was very soon broken up, along with my easel, bag, etc.

Tojours,
Claude

Claude Monet, *The Villas in Bordighera*, 1884; oil on canvas; 29 x 36½ inches (73.7 x 92.4 cm). © 2008 Dover Publicaionts Inc.

Claude Monet, *Etretat, Rough Sea*, 1883; oil on canvas; 32 x 39½ inches (81 x 100 cm) © 2008 Dover Publications Inc.

Imagine Monet soaking wet, his beard colored with oil paints, and you can understand his determination!

Giverny, Japan, and

"My garden is my most beautiful masterpiece." — Claude Monet

In 1883, Monet rented a house in Giverny. He was 43 years old and would spend another 43 years living at Giverny — literally half of his life! He purchased the property in 1890. He was lucky to find a home to accommodate Alice and her four daughters, as well as his own two sons and his artistic needs. It was a cheerful, friendly home. He liked to receive his artist friends at Giverny, which was only a day excursion out of Paris.

The house was painted pink to complement the Japanese cherry blossoms when they bloom. Japanese prints adorned the walls in abundance. Monet's Garden is a wonder of color, planned by him the way one designs a huge painting. He imported a vast array of floral species to realize his vision. In Monet's own words, "My garden is my most beautiful masterpiece."

Ando Hiroshige, *The Taiko Bridge and Yūshii Hill in Meguro*; from the series "100 Famous Places in Edo." 1857. Nishike-e, 34 x 23 cm. © 2008 Dover Publications, Inc.

Ando Hiroshige, *Fuji from Mio-No Matsubara*. Colored print, 13¼ x 8¾ inches. Collection of The Newark Museum, John Cotton Dana Collection, Inv.: 00.123. The Newark Museum, Newark, New Jersey. Photo Credit: The Newark Museum / Art Resource, NY

the Series Paintings

Monet's art is often associated with "series paintings." The haystacks or grainstacks — a theme that could hardly be less intriguing to the average eye — became a great source of inspiration through Monet's perception. The grainstacks, which stood in a field near his Giverny home, are regarded as the beginning of the series paintings — even though his earlier work showed repeated interest in a subject, such as the Gare Saint-Lazare train station paintings. The grainstacks were painted 25 times, showing the change of light according to time of day, season, and weather conditions.

Japanese artists also worked in "series." One of the best known images for Westerners is *The Great Wave*, by Hokusai. It is part of the series "36 Views of Mt. Fuji." Hiroshige also produced a series of the same name, as well as "The 53 Stations of the Tokaido Road."

As you can see on these pages, the Japanese concern with seasons, the beauty of the commonplace, love of nature, and the delight in outdoor scenes echo the essence of Monet's art. The influence of Japanese art on Monet is inarguable — particularly in his gardens at Giverny. His Japanese Footbridge was among his favorite places from which to paint.

See "Timing is Everything" in the Activity Pond, page 31

Claude Monet, *Grainstacks at Giverny, Sunset*, 1888–89; oil on canvas; 31 x 25½ inches (81 x 65 cm). Dover Publications, Inc.

Claude Monet, *Grainstacks, White Frost Effect*, 1889; oil on canvas; 25⅝ x 36¼ inches (65 x 92 cm). Dover Publications, Inc.

Claude Monet, *Poplars (Summer)*, 1891; oil on canvas; 36⅛ x 28¾ inches (92 x 73 cm). © 2008 Dover Publications, Inc.

Claude Monet, *The Poplars, Three Trees, Fall*, 1891; oil on canvas; 36⅝ x 29⅛ inches (93 x 74.1 cm). © 2008 Dover Publications, Inc.

Claude Monet, *Wind Effect, Poplar Series*, 1891; oil on canvas. © 2008 Dover Publications, Inc.

Cathedrals and Japanese Gardens

Claude Monet, *Rouen Cathedral*, 1894; oil on canvas; 26 x 39⅜ inches (65.8 x 100.1 cm). © 2008 Dover Publications, Inc.

Series would dominate Monet's approach to Impressionism from this point forward and in so doing, further advance the principles of the movement itself. Monet is the figure who most personifies the meaning of Impressionism. The eighth and final Impressionist Exhibit was held in June of 1886. Monet's mature work would establish him as a brilliant colorist, spectacular en plein air or landscape painter and founder of Western "Series" paintings. The search for inspiration made a traveler of him. A trip to the French region of Normandy yielded the town of Rouen. Its venerable attraction is a proud, old church. Monet rented a room across from the cathedral and began his series of 30 versions of the building at various times and over a period of many days. In *Rouen Cathedral, Full Sunlight*, we see the interaction between the sun's direct rays and the building's crusty façade, which seems to be baking like bread in an oven. The church's natural stones are as responsive to the climate elements as living matter, not as merely passive architecture.

Monet also visited Brittany, a remote area of France with primal landscape. *The Manneporte at Etretat II* has some of the qualities of the Rouen Cathedral. It has the monumentality of a cathedral forged by natural forces. Monet is clearly in his element. The grand arch, almost like a megalith in its appearance, represents the fortitude of nature. Once again, we can marvel at Monet's painterly description of the precise locations to which he journeyed.

Claude Monet, *Rouen Cathedral, Façade, (Gray day)*, 1894; oil on canvas, 39⅜ x 25⅝ inches (100 x 65 cm). © 2008 Dover Publications, Inc.

Claude Monet, *The Manneporte, Etretat, II*, 1886; oil on canvas; 32 x 25¾ inches (81.3 x 65.4 cm). © 2008 Dover Publications, Inc.

IDEA

The world is filled with wonderful structures, both in the built and natural environment. Draw façades and other forms that intrigue you in your sketchbook!

Monet received permission to have the River Epte redirected to his Giverny property. It was a small river which was situated near the Seine. Local farmers were initially skeptical about their artist-gardener neighbor and his ways but soon came to accept him and his ideas. Water was the essential centerpiece of Monet's interest — it enabled his now famous lily pond. He would paint at his pond for hours, under the shade of an umbrella fitted to his easel. He recorded the reflections of the clouds, the movement of the water, and said, "To understand my water lilies, I planted them…I grew them without ever thinking of painting… then suddenly it dawned on me how wonderful my pond was, and I reached for my palette."

Claude Monet, *Water Lilies and Japanese Bridge*, 1899; oil on canvas; 35⅖ x 36⅗ inches (89.9 x 93 cm). © 2008 Dover Publications, Inc.

Shofuso Japanese House and Garden, Philadelphia, PA

The 1880s and 1890s would bring success to Monet. A one-man show was held. Art dealer Durand-Ruel acquired most of Monet's paintings for buyers in 1881. Many paintings were exhibited — 40 in America in 1886 — and in Paris, there was the Exposition Universelle, where Monet exhibited with Manet and Pissarro. The Eiffel tower made its appearance at this big event! Monet also shared a major exhibition with sculptor Auguste Rodin in 1889. Things were definitely looking up!

Claude Monet, *Water-Lily Pond*, Giverny, 1919; oil on canvas; 39¾ x 78¾ inches (101 x 200 cm). © 2008 Dover Publications, Inc.

THE INTREPID

Monet and his second wife, Alice, at the Piazza San Marco in Venice.

There were pigeons all over us and I was wincing a bit with fright. But the picture was taken the moment they flew away.

Monet bought a car in 1900 so he could drive over the Alps to San Moritz in the heart of winter.

This is Monet's palette!

The Four Principles

Monet had four Impressionist concepts which he repeated again and again in his work.

Motif: Motifs were very important to both Monet and Cézanne. Put simply, motifs are the essence of a particular scene or theme. Motifs have a special appeal, such as the cliffs in Etretat or the train station at Gare Saint Lazare. For Cézanne, it was Mont Saint Victoire at Aix-en-Provence, France.

Effet: Effet (effect) is the way light changes subjects (motifs). Think about the haystacks and how different one looks from the other depending on the time of day or weather condition.

Féerique: A term that means "fairylike" and describes "special effects" caught in paint. At this, Monet is a magician. Think about the way the stone of the Rouen Cathedral appears to dissolve before our eyes. Féerique is seen in the painting of the Grand Canal (at right) which seems to have a mystical and exotic appearance. Monet is a master of illusion, yet everything is real!

Décoration: This word does not have the same meaning as in English, which could refer to wallpaper or giftwrap. In French, décoration describes art as it is installed as a mural or an artistically styled stage set design. See page 28 for Monet's Grandes Décorations, *The Water Lilies*.

"As for the colors I use, what's so interesting about that? I don't think one could paint better or more brightly with another palette. The most important thing is to know how to use the colors. Their choice is a matter of habit. In short, I use white lead, cadmium yellow, vermillion, madder, cobalt blue, chrome green. That's all."
— Claude Monet

Monet understood Chevreul's Law of Simultaneous Contrast, which states that when two complementary colors are placed against one another, the result is a powerful optical mixture in the eye of the viewer. Color theory was critical to Impressionism.

TRAVELER

IDEA — Do you have a favorite place to go—or skyline that amazes you? See Activity Pond on pages 30-31!

Since the 18th century, Italy has been a destination for artists, poets, aristocrats, and tourists. In 1908, Monet and Alice made the trip to Rome, Florence, and Venice. It did not take long before Monet began painting the marvels that he saw before him. This canal scene is a fine example of not only his established skill with water; it also is a classic example of "féerique" (see page 26).

Monet also returned to London to do a series of the Houses of Parliament. Voilà, c'est féerique! The illusion that the buildings sit on a river of fire is simply a reflection of the sunset.

Claude Monet, *The Grand Canal*, 1908; oil on canvas; 28¾ x 36⅓ inches (73 x 92 cm). © 2008 Dover Publications, Inc.

Claude Monet, *The Houses of Parliament, Sunset*, 1904; oil on canvas; 32 x36⅓ inches (81 x 92 cm). © 2008 Dover Publications, Inc.

Monet traveled incessantly to find his ideal motifs, effects, and décorations. True to the Realist belief, "I paint what I see," Monet did not invent composite pictures. His commitment to place and subject would keep him traveling his entire life.

Monet led a rich, full life. He became a legend. Yet he suffered tragedies just the same. His early years included struggles with poverty as he strived to gain recognition as a painter. He endured the death of two wives and lost his eldest son to illness. Monet's work outdoors required a hearty constitution. It would be his eyesight that would cause him the most difficulty in his later years, but even vision loss did not stop him from painting. He died at the age of 86 in 1926, and was the longest living of the Impressionist painters. The Prime Minister of France, Georges Clemenceau, was in attendance at his intimate funeral at his beloved Giverny.

The Sistine Chapel of

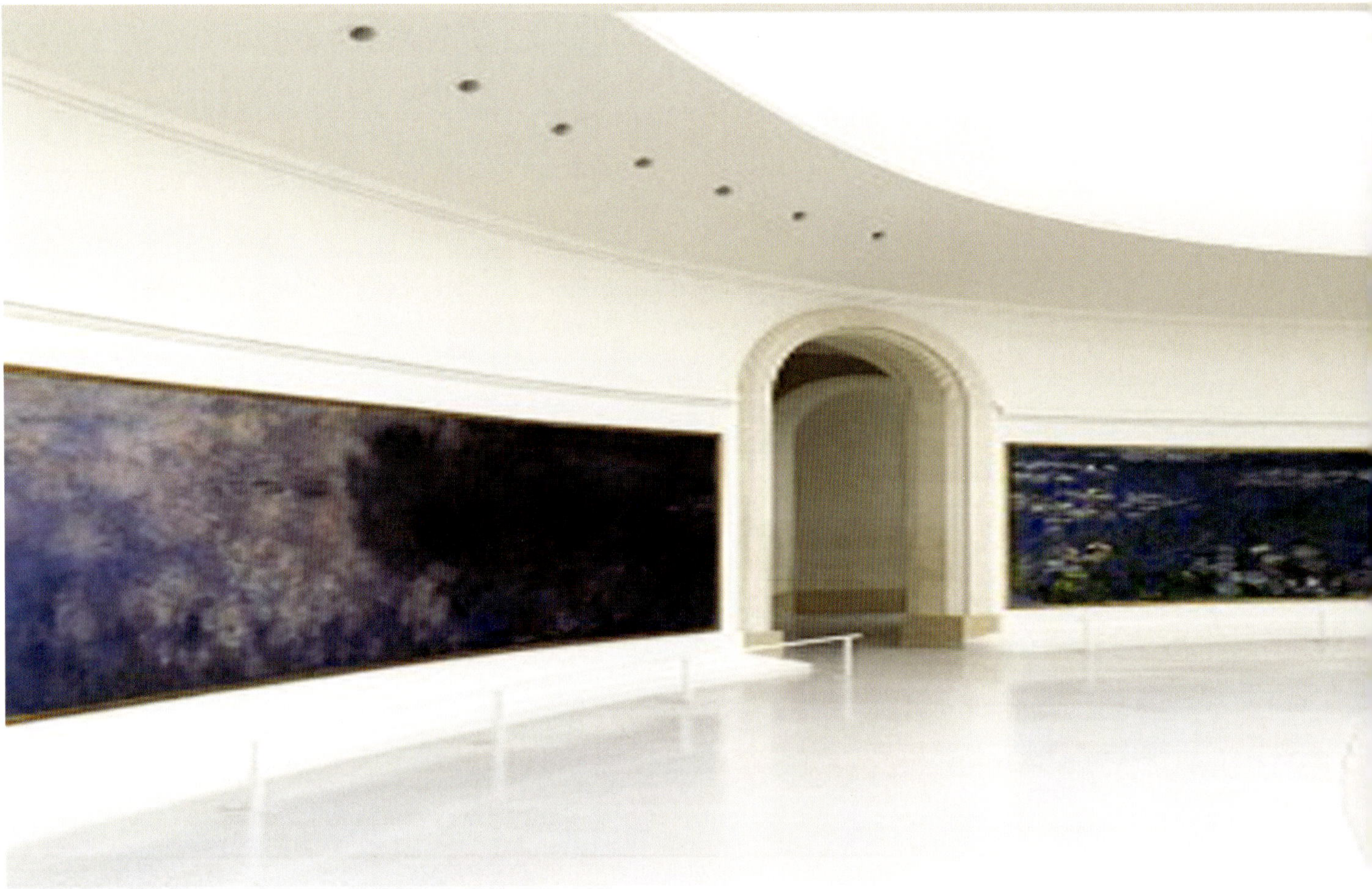

Le Cycle des Nyphéas (The Cycle of the Water Lilies)

Dear and close friend,

I am on the eve of finishing two decorative panels which I wish to sign on the day of Victory, and am asking you to offer them to the State... It's not much, but it's the only way I have of taking art into the victory.

Claude Monet

Photo: Henri Maneul.

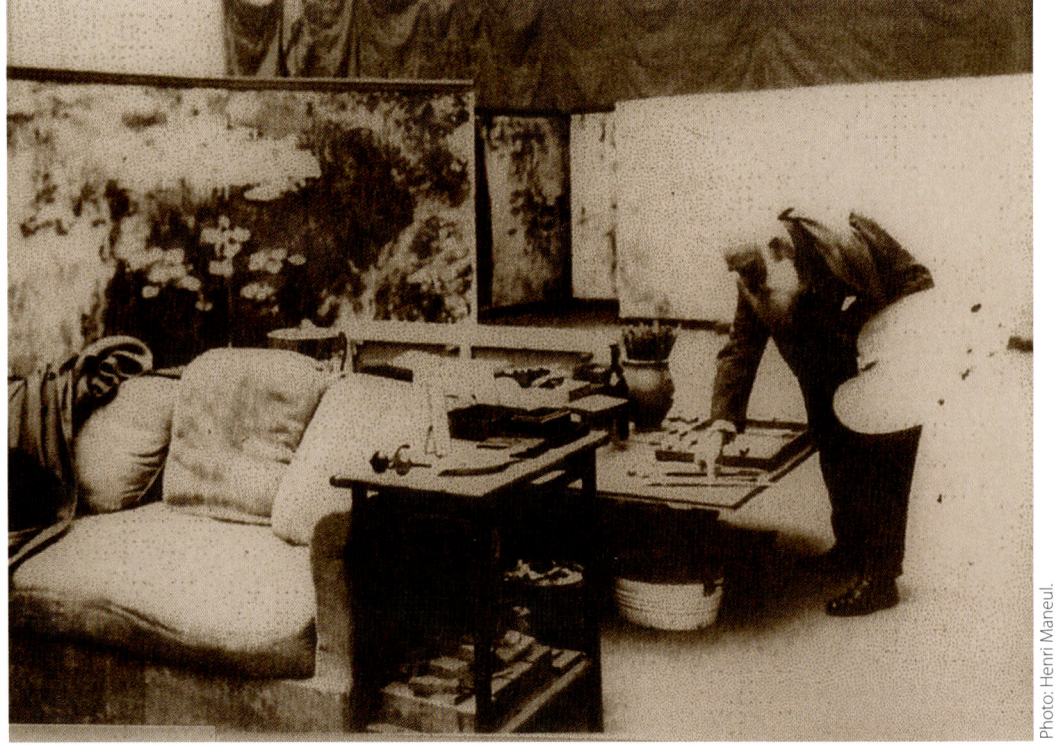

Claude Monet at work on Les Nymphéas Cycle. Monet prepares more than forty panels for the Musée de l'Orangerie.

Impressionism

Late in his life, Monet was commissioned by Prime Minister Clemenceau to produce a project called Les Grandes Decorations. Twelve vast canvasses would cover two expansive elliptical rooms. The two motifs were Les Nyphéas (Water Lilies) and Weeping Willows. His source of inspiration was Giverny — its gardens and pond. The canvasses were removed from their stretchers and were affixed to the curved walls. Unfortunately, Monet did not live to see the unveiling of the paintings in 1927. His wishes to have the light directed in a particular manner to illuminate the motifs probably would have pleased him greatly.

If you ever have the opportunity to visit this incredible installation you will feel as though you have been submerged into the embrace of Monet's precious water lilies.

The textures, brilliant colors, and openness of the water lily motifs convey the sensations that Monet intended.

ACTI

YOUR OWN GIVERNY
Giverny was the realization of Monet's dream. He put enormous efforts into planning his garden which required six full-time gardeners. You can have your own version of Giverny by simply collecting garden magazines, seed catalogs, and photographs of flowers which will then by "planted" as individual collages. You might want to include the footbridge for contrast. Just as Monet planted flowers of many colors, tones, and textures, think about how your flowers and plants will look in your own Giverny!

Claude Monet, *Suzanne Reading and Blanche Painting by the* inches (91.5 x 98 cm). © 2008 Dover Publications, Inc.

THE CHARM OF THE LITTLE FACADE
The French people love an artistic touch when it comes to the arrangement of even the little grocery store window. A great activity is to recreate a store front on a Paris street by using the bottom side of a shoe box and drawing the contents of the store on the inside of the box. It is about art, architecture, and food. C'est bon.

The Water Lilies Cycle at the Russell Byers Charter School in Philadelphia was a collaborative effort — the older students painted the water and the lily pads, and the younger children created the three-dimensional lilies.

LE PIQUE-NIQUE
Did you know the French say they invented the idea of the picnic? Have an art picnic in your classroom with paper plates on which you illustrate your favorite food(s). Or have students research foods from different countries and create a collage on a paper plate. Place all the dishes on a checkered plastic cloth. A baguette of bread and fromage (cheese) are popular French picnic foods.

VITY POND

Claude Monet, *Grainstacks at Giverny, Sunset*, 1888–89; oil on canvas; 31 x 25⅝ inches. © 2008 Dover Publications, Inc.

EN PLEIN AIR PAINTING
En plein air simply means outdoors; it is a wonderful change of pace for a teacher to take students out of the classroom with sketchbooks or paper and a flat portable surface. Pick a pleasant day and go to a nearby park or even your schoolyard. Find your view. Using colored pencils (or watercolor pencils or tempera) "paint what you see," as Monet would say.

Marsh at Giverny, 1887; oil on canvas; 36 x 38⅝

Edouard Manet, *Monet in his Floating Studio*, 1874, oil on canvas, 82.7 x 105 cm. Bildarchiv Preussischer Kulturbesitz / Art Resource, NY

PAINTING A PAINTING IN A PAINTING
On this page there are two examples of painting a painting in a painting. To compose a picture in a picture, a self-portrait with an empty frame behind you is a sure bet. Portrait painters use this idea often as it creates visual space. Try it using paint or markers.

Claude Monet, *Grainstacks, White Frost Effect*, 1889; oil on canvas; 25⅝ x36⅝ inches. © 2008 Dover Publications, Inc.

TIMING IS EVERYTHING
Timing is everything when you paint a series. Notice how Monet has studied these grainstacks in different times of day and in different seasons. Try your own series. Start by folding a piece of paper into four quarters. Select an object outside your classroom window such as a tree, flower, branch, or side of a building. Draw it at different times of day or in different conditions. Aren't the differences in light, shadow, and color surprising? Monet thought so too!

CITY REFLECTIONS
Do you have a favorite place near water… perhaps a favorite skyline? Monet loved the London skyline and the reflection of the Houses of Parliament in the river Thames. You might find beauty in the city lights as they reflect on a river or lake. Just as Monet sometimes included industry, you can consider the same. Wherever your favorite place — include a body of water in your artwork where you can show reflections. Use oil pastel or colored chalks. Dip chalks in a small cup of water as you use them — the effect will be that of a painting — and no dust!

DON'T FORGET TO WRITE: MAIL ART
As long as there has been mail, there has been mail art, which can take many forms. Today, people worry that letter writing may become a lost art. Write a letter on a creative page (maps make wonderful stationery) — maybe a letter to Monet about one of his paintings. Tell him what you think about it and how the painting makes you feel. Feel free to include doodles or illustrations.

Look for other activities throughout the book

31

Travels with Monet is recommended for art teachers, students, artists, classroom teachers of all grades, college courses, museum educators, art and nature lovers, journal keepers, and of course, travelers.

Open air artists do portraits, too! Just visit Montmartre in Paris, France, and you shall see.